Just Bee You

"Heddie J." Simmons

A Poetic Ministree, Inc.
APoeticMinistree.com

ISBN: 9781648585845

For Worldwide Distribution, Printed in the USA.

Dedication

To my Heavenly Father who has never left me for whatever I have done, is doing or could ever do. Thank you for your Love, which has allowed me to J.U.S.T. B.E.E. Heddie.

To My Family:
To my Husband Sylvester whose support goes beyond words.
Thank you for your patience and tolerence.
To my children, Karmen and Nehemiah,
thank you both for listening, agreeing and disagreeing
with all of my inspired ideas.

To the men and women who have given of themselves just so I could be myself, thank you for your prayers and actions that has shaped my very being.

To My Prayer Partner:
Thank you for being a friend.

To the one who always tells me "No Matter what it looks like, God is in Charge," *thank You for your never ending Wisdom.*

To You, the Reader:
May the words written on these pages help you *Just Bee You.*

To My Publisher:
To Gail Moss, The Poetical Evangelist, I will forever have the memory of you walking into mere obedience. Thank You.

Preface

Have you ever just felt stuck? I have for some time now. After the death of my mother in 1980, I have always felt like there was more to my life at the age of 14. I went to college, got married, had children and was given this gift of Poetry. I knew I was called by God but I still felt stuck. I kept hearing 'just be you' all of my life. Then one day, it hit me. All of my poetical pieces screamed Being.

JUST BEE YOU came about because we are to DO the work required of us that makes us unique. In other words, we should Be as Busy As a BEE. We must BEE - Believe Especially and Expect God's Business within us. Time will Bring all things together.

Here is my analogy. The Bumble Bee is to life physically as we Be in life Spiritually. Let me explain. No fruit or vegetable arrives in your favorite store without being pollinated by a BEE. When we Become in the spirit, we live fulfilled productive lives not just for ourselves but those around us as we all BEcome.

You the Reader are **Justified Under Salvation To Believe and Expect Especially Your Own Uniqueness**. We need each other like our food requires pollination from the Bees. May I say it again, J.U.S.T. B.E.E. Y.O.U Enjoy and find yourself in each Poem and Get as Busy as that Bee.

I Bring You Peace.

Acknowledgements

All Pictures by Heddie J's Private Collection except:

Book Cover and graphic with the poem on page 38 by Artist Devonna Arrington @artistically_d

Picture on page 20 by Sayuri Smith-Timmons, CPS of Mass Exodus Life Coaching LLC

Table of Contents

WHAT IS YOUR LAND

Do You Know What **Your** Land is all about in You
Do you Really Realize that Your Land is exactly What you do
A Preacher's Land are the ears that Her Words fall upon
Words that can cause Kayos or Bring Calm

A Poet may call oneself a simple old poet
Her words so soothing, her **Land** and she doesn't even know it
As the Pen hits the paper, the Words are just Right
Her land is just Flowing without ever a fight

A Nurse is a Nurse but her Land is much more
Sick people are not just sick, there is more to be told
Emotions fly high when you are stuck in a bed
The Nurse's Land here is getting the Emotions and
Mental mind Fed

The song says, "This Land is Your Land, This Land Is My Land"
But in Reality, My land is not Your Land, only according to man
What is your Land? What did God Grace You to Do
Are you walking in it Proudly or are you Stumbling and
Feeling Blue

Your Land **is** not just a piece of Acquired property
But to do what God has Skillfully Graced you to do
If you have Never Ever Seen your Land
Then Talk to God and Get his **Predestined** Plan

What is Your Land
Is It According to God or Is It According To Man?

9

DEAD OR ALIVE

We walk around with the word on us only for a show
We go to church on Sunday not even realizing Service as we go
You passed by a car broke down with the people standing by their ride
No, you don't stop, offer a phone, going to church Dead or Alive

There is no one around, behind closed doors, you stump your toe
The choice words which exits your mouth only God knows
You go to the movies to see a flick X-Rated, Oh My
Dead for your Soul
No one around to see you watching, laughing enjoying a dead show

Monday morning on your job, you tossed and turned, not enough sleep
You woke up, but to what, no word in your soul, nothing to keep

You left your house no prayers said
You dressed yourself Alive or Dead

Rush hour traffic got you late
A wreck ahead a tragic fate
You said no prayer for that poor old soul
You could have helped to make him whole

Dead lives lead dead trails
Nothing to follow but attempted fails

You wonder why **YOU** can't get ahead
You wake with no word, completely dead
So **Try** the life and be Alive
Try the faith that's full of **LIFE**

Now I ask you as you awaken each day
Dead or Alive, you Choose Which Way.

PARTAKE OF ME

What placed you in that state you are in right now
What is keeping you from calmness in your mind
The answer is right there, it always really was
You refuse to partake of me only just because

You awaken each new day to a task always ahead
You still don't praise my Name, No **I AM** not dead
I held you last night in my arms and kept you free from harm
But still you refuse to partake of me, Should I be Alarmed

I have all the answers when you know not where to go
Yet, you still know nothing and try to run this show
When you daily need new comfort, I will send my Holy Spirit
I'm constantly calling your name
But you never seem to hear it

Partake of me…I'm the only one to give you rest
I have all of your answers to help you pass life's test
When you feel pain and turmoil, I will give you Peace
When you think you're frustrated, I will say trouble, Cease

I'm always talking to you through others, yes all the Time
I'm always giving you answers with my word and a sign
I want you to take me daily all the time so you will see
I am always **Here** for you, if you will just Partake of Me.

JUST BEE YOU

NEVER BE ANOTHER

There will Never BE Another Me
Yes, I will BE the Best Me That I will Ever BE
There Will Never BE Another You
You Will BE the Best You In All that You Are Destined to Do

There will Never BE Another You
No One Will Ever Do what God Has Graced **YOU** to Do
What is it That Has You So Scared
You Must Realize You are Already Graced

There will Never BE Another Time As Now
Walk into Your God-Given Power
You have Keys to Unlock Those bound
Why are you Just Waiting and Not Pulling It Down

There **WILL** Never BE Another Today
Not Tomorrow nor Next Week, There is no Way
The Time is Now All Wrapped Up in Your Loins
What Else do you Need to Just Get You Going

There Will Never BE Another Power
Just Grab on to Him in this Very Hour
Take His Love and Still **Keep Going** Farther
I'm Telling You Now, There Will Never BE Another.

WHATEVER

Whatever is in Your Heart…Feel It

Whatever is in Your Soul…BE It

Whatever is in **Your** Mind…Conceive It

Whatever is in Your **Life**…Live It

Whatever it is your Heart Desires…Receive it

Whatever Comes Your Way…Deal With It

Whatever God Has Called You to Do…**Become It.**

Whatever

FIND YOUR FLOW

Find it Fast… Find It Slow…It Really doesn't

matter how, Just know

You must Never remain still in any of your Ways

Find your Flow in God for much needed days

You do have a current…Are you Moving in it

Or are you Standing Still not using your Will

Find you Flow…in **God** you must BE

Find it soon…So God can Fit every need

Find it…Don't worry about Anything Else

Find it…So you will always BE at your Best

Find it…Find Your Flow and Take it no matter

Where You Go. Find it…Find Your Flow.

ACCEPT WHO YOU ARE

Stop Fighting the very thing I have Placed in you to BE
Stop Listening to Others Who Don't Want to See
That You Are That Person In What You Feel
Accept This Truth and Shine, BE Healed

Stop Telling Others Your Dreams Only Because
Those you Tell Can't Think Otherwise
It Does take Wisdom to Sit with the Father
It Proves to Others Why Sitting Is not a Bother

Realize Now How Special You are to BE
The Father Created you so Well to See
Accepting Who You Are Proves Your Trust in Him
You Accepting Yourself is How You Win

Let This BE the last Day You Feel this Way
No More Running Away from **YOURSELF** I say
Even When You Feel Bent out of Shape
No Matter What, You Will feel More than Great

Doors will Open and You Will SEE
The Importance of God in You Waiting to BE
You Will Find a Freedom Sparkling Like a Star
You will see your Purpose Accepting Who You Are.

JUST BEE YOU

YOU ARE NEVER ALONE

We are so Carefully Thought of You See
God has Angles over our Beings Mightily
They Minister to us in Their own Given Ways
They Even Bring Messages on needed Days

An Angel Told Joseph to take Mary as His Wife
For He Had not Touched Mary or Fathered that Life
That Mary Carried seeded by the Holy Spirit
When Angels Do Speak, **Your** Spirit Will Hear It

Angels are Given Charge over us you Know
They even Deliver Messages to help us Flow
Occasionally they are Visible and then some are not
It depends on their **Assignments** they receive from God

Sometimes we **Are** not Aware of Entertaining Them
When They are in our Presence **from** start to end
It is Usually after the Fact when the Day has gone by
We think Back on the situation and then understand Why

So know in your heart and Remember from now on
God is Always with you, You are Never Alone.

GETTING YOUR INSIDE OUTSIDE

What I have placed in **You** Definitely **Must** Come out
The Method others use will only make you shout
It is that on the inside that truly does matter
This hard life you have, was never meant for shatter

The Pain, the Hurt, the Tears, the Cruel Feeling of Rejection
Open your Eyes and See that your Inside is Under Construction
"I" Your Maker has placed a Mighty and Powerful Word in You
But Your Inside Must Come Out, to Finish Up My Truth

What I have placed in you, no You can't Dare Keep to Yourself
Those highly Spiritual Gifts were Made for Someone Else
When a true man of God, truly Preaches from the Pulpit
Those really Listening are set Free from the Words Spoken

Your life is Exploding with the Inside trying to Get Out
Once you Start to get This, Others can truly Shout
Your Insides are your Gifts that God Skillfully Placed in Thee
Open up, Let Him out and Let God's Truth set Others Free

Stop Hiding Yourself and Let Your True Desires Go
Open up and let Why you Feel, Be What You Powerfully Know
No, You Truly have Nothing to Ever Really Hide
Now You Know Why You Need to Get Your Inside Outside.

BE

It is Time to Stop Playing with Yourself
BE Who You Are, You do Have help
BE the YOU God Created You to BE
Understand Your Wealth, Your True Identity

Identify with Christ who Intercedes for You
The One who was Flogged and Bled for You
The One who Sits With God Pleading For You

BE and **Believe** there is Nothing You Can't Do
Yes Those Things Ordained Only For You
That Sound in the Earth You are to Produce
You're Not to Copy Others But Mimic Only You

Now is the Time to Show Why You Were Born
You Just Need to Believe **and** not Daily Morn
This is the Day That the Lord Has Made
BE That Created You, while Moving Out of Fear

Expect New Things Never Done Before
Expect Your Own Uniqueness to Explore
Expect the Excitement of Finding You
BELIEVE and EXPECT This Vessel Called **YOU.**

YOUR IMAGINATION

Let's recall the **Images** you had as a child
For some of you, this Has Been awhile
You Must Agree that those same Images were Strong
They have been what has shaped you All along

In Shaping I mean wanting to Be that Very Thing
That You Somehow Work in now from the Beginning
Dreams of Being A Doctor or Even a Nurse
These Images You Repeatedly Rehearsed

If You **are** Truly Created in the Image of God
Those Images you Have are actually God's Words
Your Purpose on this Earth Placed Within You
The Reason You Live And What You Do

Sometimes those images are Very Clear
And At other Times, they Come from nowhere
They are the Word of God **From** God into your Being
Your Purpose on this Earth just As you are Seeing

God took the Time to Place Himself in You
Through Your Image, Showing You What to do
Rethink those Times and go Back to See
How your Imagination, Truly Must BE.

JUST BEE YOU

YOUR WORDS

Ever Wonder at Times how the **Words** We Speak
Can Make one Feel Strong and other times Weak
It is Because of the Tongue and Its Given Authority
What You Say no Matter When, Will One Day BE

Yes This Muscle Placed within Your Mouth
Can Make you Cry, Dance, Sing and even Shout
Death can come from the Words you Choose to Speak
Bring Down Kings and Queens while on their Knees

Then On the Other Hand, Life Could BE so Sweet
Like Roses Meeting A Vase as a Special Treat
Start to Honor the Power of What You Say
Exercise the Power of Life as You Speak Today

See the Power of Your Words Daily as you Proclaim
The Goodness of God as You Call on His Name
Live the Positive Words That Are So Full of Life
Experience Eating of This Fruit with unwanted Strife

Speak Life Daily so You Could Truly See
How the **Power** Of Your Words Will Live and BE
Know Your Spoken Words Will Come to Past
Just Make Them Positive and Forever They Will Last.

YOUR MIND

Each person reading these Words today
Has a choice to make As They Think Which Way
Your Thought Process is vital in Serving the King
Where Your Mind is, Establishes Your Being

When One Thinks of the Goodness of the Lord
Your Entire Being is Affected and Never Board
Your Mind Was Never Given to BE Wasted
Making Individual Necessary Decisions

We are Told to BE of one Mind to have a Willing Mind
Which Allows A Peaceful Flow living Among Mankind
Being Still Allows the Will of the Father to BE A Father
Stillness Settles Your Mind and One Hears Better

Transformation Starts to Take Place From Within
One is Renewed From the Inside, Freshness Begins
Which Allows God's Good, Perfect and Acceptable Will
Renewing The Mind When You Stop and BE **Still**

So Make Up Your Mind and Let This Power Start **Within**
BE Of Good Cheer as you Draw Closer To God Nearer
Make Your Mind and Allow This Concept Today
By Committing your Thoughts,
God Will Establish Your Ways.

JUST BEE YOU

YOUR ACCEPTANCE

I never thought I would Ever See the Day
When Life As we Knew It, Is Taken Away
I Used to Wonder When a Stadium was Packed
How Many of Those Souls **Consider** God as a Fact

My mind would Wonder How People Could
Be So Cruel Laughing at God as they Did
We Are Told to Wear A Mask Everywhere we Go
Even Doing That, We Don't Know For Sure

Yet, I do Know One Thing That Will Never Change
Even During Corona, **God** Will Forever Reign
He Still Gives us Life when Life Looks so Strange
We must Realize Where We are to Rearrange

Either Accept What you See or Faithfully Believe
You are not Doomed When You've Accepted the Keys
Given to Us to Fight and Truly Use Faithfully
Keys Open Doors Which Does Represent Authority

Your Acceptance of God is a Powerful Start
You Must know Who He is Within Your Heart
There is Nothing That Will Separate You From God
You Accepting Him Makes Living Today not so Hard.

JUST BEE YOU

Your Land is Predestined as You Try Life
You are **Justified Under Salvation** not Strife
God is Saying, 'I Am Here' **to** Your Soul Everyday
You Must Keep Going, **Believe** Whatever Comes Your Way

You Will **Exceptionally** Find God Accepting Yourself
Expect and Know Your Assignments are From God with Wealth
You Must Stop Hiding to Believe and **Expect**
Those Images Are From God That you Work With

Believing and Knowing as You Exercise Power
Being Still Within is How You Win in Every Hour
Fear will not Paralyze You as You Move Along I Say
You Have Power, Love and that Sound Mind Today

BE As Busy As That Bee as You Work **Your** Land
You have Help With God Lending His Powerful Hand
Own What is Yours and Take it Where ever You May Go
Your **Uniqueness** Must Come Through, This You Must Show.

THE ABC'S OF BEING

If You Want to BEE, Consider Using Your ABC's.

Stop...

Allowing Others to Use Up Your Time.
Blaming Others for Your Own Downfall.
Creating Chaos Within Your Own Space.
Dwelling Among Liars.
Eating From the Wrong Plate.
Forcing Yourself Into Someone Else's Mold.
Gaining the Prospective of a Thief.
Holding on to the Past Choking Your Future.
Ignoring Your Own Potential.
Juggling the Truth with False Realities.
Killing Your Own Destiny With Fear.
Looking Up to False Images.
Managing Others at Your own Expense.
Nagging.
Opening Closed Doors Already Shut.
Pushing Your Own Uniqueness Away.
Questioning Your God Given Gifts.
Running the Same Dead Ends.
Sabotaging Your Own Dreams.
Trailblazing Another's Coat Tail.
Underestimating Your God Given Power.
Vandalizing Your Own Belief.
Winning For the Wrong Reasons.
X-rating Yourself to Foolishness.
Yielding Yourself to Dead Situations Repeatedly.
Zapping The Life Out Of Your Gifts.

ABOUT THE AUTHOR

Heddie J. Simmons was born in Georgetown, South Carolina second of five children. She knew she wanted to be a Nurse at the age of four when her mother was diagnosed with cancer in 1970. Her mother ended up dying in 1980 while Heddie was a freshman in high school.

Heddie suffered from severe Migraine headaches, which caused uncontrolled seizures while on daily doses of Dilantin. Words were spoken that somehow Heddie refused to believe as she daily struggled mentally to live. Her doctors told her that she would never live a normal life because of the seizures. Because of the power of prayer, the seizures are gone. Because of the power of words, she became hope for others even after a failed suicide attempt.

Heddie was given the gift of poetry two weeks after dreaming the events of September 11. Nineteen years later, (which represents faith) JUST BEE YOU is finally birthed using the power of words. Each poem delivers a message within a message by divinely inspiring the reader. You are **Justified Under Salvation To Believe** and **Expect Especially Your Own Uniqueness**. In other words, *JUST BEE YOU*.